First published in Australia 2023 by DC Imaging, Toowoomba, Queensland, 4350

Photography copyright David Martinelli

Hidden Treasure images photographed by David Martinelli
Cover concept: photography and design by David Martinelli

Book design by D.C. Imaging ABN 88 426 063 633
2 Princess Street, Toowoomba, Queensland, Australia
+61 487192364

ISBN: 978-0-9943125-4-9

Hidden Treasure

on Australia's Northern Coastline

by David Martinelli

Acknowledgement

Special opportunities come, but once in a life-time. For this one, I am grateful to David Stanfield of the charity 'Free People', and the family of Marvis, who extended an invitation to visit the Island to photograph and (video) record a special event.

The production of this book was greatly assisted advice by Ken Ball. I would also like to express my gratitude to Greg Strahorn, Erin Byle and Gerald Chapman, who gave of their time to proof read the text and providing valuable feedback. A special mention to my wife Cathy, who is a constant (moral) support in these sorts of projects.

INTRODUCTION

Elcho Island is situated on the northern coastline of Australia, five hundred kilometres east of Darwin, (known to locals as Galiwin'ku, which is the indigenous name for the island and the township). The beach scenes captured in this publication is situated five kilometres west of the Galiwin'ku township.

On the second day, a visit was made to the local Elder Richard, to signal our arrival on the island. He granted us permission to walk freely and photograph our time on the beach.

The visual stimuli was overwhelming, from the colour and coarse texture of the sand, to the reflections on the rain soaked sand. From the developing (late season) storm on the horizon, to the presence of the three dingos playing in the shallows. To the endless expansion of exposed vibrant purple coloured rocks, close to the shore line, and the surprise appearance of the young dingos frolicking in the shallows.

Australia - An Island Nation

Australia is the world's largest island continent with a coastlne of 25,760km. Well over sixty percent of the coastline is uninhabited. This is primarily in northern Queensland; the Northern Territory and along the majority of the coast of Western Australia.

There are 8,222 islands within the maritime borders of Australia. There are over eight hundred wislands are off the northern coastline. They are scattered across the empty space between where the Territory ends, and Indonesia begins.

There are fifteen major islands off the coast of Arnhem Land. Arnhem Land is a vast wilderness area in the northeast corner of Australia's Northern Territory, defined by rocky escarpments, gorges, rivers and waterfalls. It is home to the traditional landowners, the Yolngu people.

The region consists of the eastern half of the large peninsula that forms the northernmost portion of the Northern Territory. The region, with a total area of about 37,000 square miles (95,900 square km), consists of a ruggedly dissected plateau and associated lowlands lying between the Roper and Alligator rivers. The coast of Arnhem Land extends from Van Diemen Gulf and the Cobourg Peninsula eastward to Gove Peninsula, the Gulf of Carpentaria and Groote Eylandt.

Arnhem Land derives its name from Cape Arnhem. In April 1644, Tasman named Arnhem Land after the Dutch vessel "Arnhem" which explored the area in 1623. Cape Arnhem, derives its name from one of the two Dutch ships "Pera" and "Arnhem" which in April 1623 proceeded in company along the south coast of New Guinea.

Map of ARNHEM LAND

GARIG GUNAK BARLU NATIONAL PARK

MELVILLE ISLAND

Milikapiti
Pirlangimpi

Nguiu
BATHURST ISLAND

COBOURG MARINE PARK

Smith Point

CROKER ISLAND

Murganella

GOULBURN ISLANDS

Warrumi

DARWIN

Maningrida

Milingimbi

Galiwinku

GOVE PENINSULA

Gunbalanya (Oenpelli)

JABIRU

ARNHEM HWY

NHULUNBUY

Ramingining

Yirrkala

Dhupuma

LITCHFIELD NATIONAL PARK

Gapuwiyak

ARNHEM LAND

STUART HWY

KAKADU HWY

KAKADU NATIONAL PARK

Balma

GROOTE EYLANDT

Daly River

PINE CREEK

CENTRAL ARNHEM RD

Bulman

Alyangula

NITMILUK (KATHERINE GORGE) NATIONAL PARK

Mainoru

KATHERINE

Numbulwar

GULF OF CARPENTARIA

RIA HWY

9

Elder Richard.

At the outskirts of town, as the bitumen ends,
and the road continues, it turns into a pothole-infested
gravel road extending for five kilometres as it follows
the contour of the coastline. It leads to a small group
of dwellings in a clearing. They are surrounded
by bushland on three sides and a secluded beach
on the western side.

Permission to walk on the beach was granted by the
local Elder Richard. As we approach, we are greeted
by two tinnies resting at the high water mark.

.

View from the rear deck of Elder's dwelling. A well worn path is visible, leading down to the secluded beach.

Descending onto the beach a panoramic view opens up. The water had receded, revealing clusters of rocks offshore.

The scene appears ordinary at first,
but as we walked along the beach.
we noticed a shimmering patch ahead,
on closer inspectection we notice a constant
stream of water, seeping from the sand,
trickling down to the water's edge, carving
little channels in the coarse, orange sand.

.

Exposed rocks of varying size and shapes appear to be randomly placed.

An old dingo leads the way onto the beach, disappearing to rest against a huge barnacle-covered rock, staring towards the shore.

Large volcanic rocks spill onto
the beach; in the distance storm
clouds amass in columns of rain.

The temperature noticeably lowers as the humidity fades. The sun still shining through as the storm continues to build over the horizon; as a light shower begins to fall.

Beyond the volcanic rocks the mangroves
appear to be steadily moving toward
the water's edge; resembling
a slow-moving caterpillar.

The storm's reflection intensifies on the rain soaked sand as the sun fades ...

Distant barking reveals two more dingos.
Noticing our presence, their inquiring bark ceases
as they play in the shallows, left behind by the receding tide.

The intense focus of this pair of dingos was astonishing, totally ignoring our presence.

This old dingo appears beside me.
His beckoning gaze demands attention.
Satisfied, he sits and stares into
the distance before lying down

on the wet sand.

"Don't come between fighting dogs", couldn't
be more of a true saying. The younger pair
suddenly turned on the old male. His submissive
behaviour quickly quelled any aggression.

The storm moves along at walking pace,
presenting a new scene with every step.
The storm clouds build and change shape.
A dingo appears in the foreground as if on queue,
following the clouds as they move.

The floral shaped storm cloud dominates the sky.
Small streams appear in the exposed sand
beyond the large rocks, as the water
continues to recede offshore.

The exposed rocks change in size,
shape and colour; from a muddy grey
they transform into an array of rich, dark,
purple hues, as the sand intenifies to an
orange tinge with the appearance of the sun.
A secluded bay comes into view as we
continue to head west on the beach.

A panoramic view of this late-season storm, as it rests over Howard Island, which is situated west of Elcho Island.

A layer of vegetation crowns this undulating rock face. The water mark clearly defined by a sharp, deep, horizontal crevice in the rock.

The deep, clear, footprints draw your attention ahead. A rock formation high above the water mark hides a special place, that has been frequented regularly for centuries. It is a place where secret men's business is conducted.

The old dingo leads the way, walking gingerly among the rocks. Finding his way into this room as if visiting an old friend, temporarily pausing before moving away.

Looking over a cluster of rocks
in this tranqil bay, as the distant
storm appears to stop and dissipate.

This young dingo cautiously steps
upon the craggy rock platform,
pausing to look out across the bay.

The older dingo joins the younger, as they both place their paws as if in a synchronized dance; moving slowly across the uneven surface.

Accepting our presence with calm disregard, the young dingo gives a slight glance before disappearing.

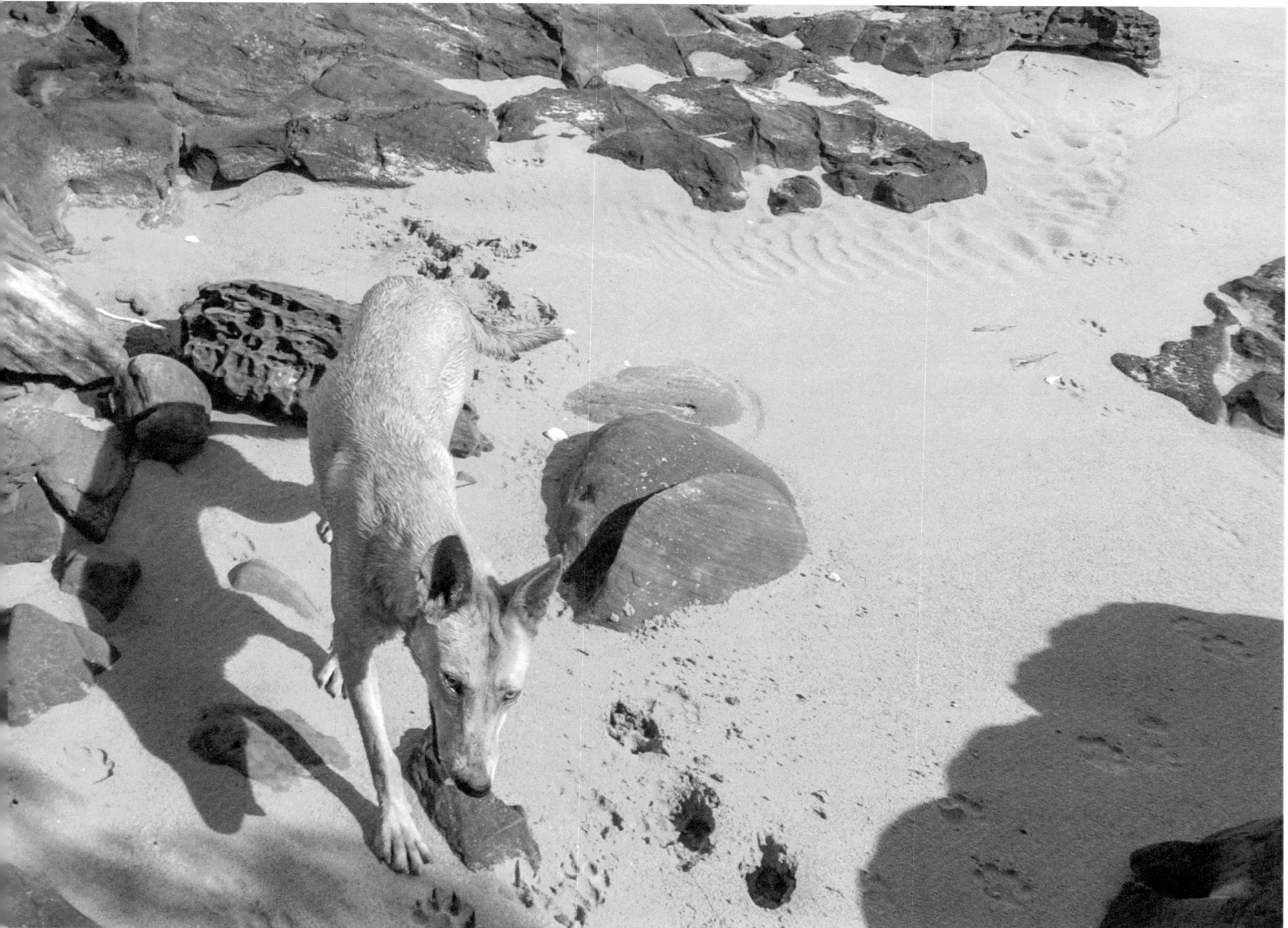

The loving look of an old friend
as he sits among the rocks.
The upturned ears and a smile
indicating a sense of contentment.

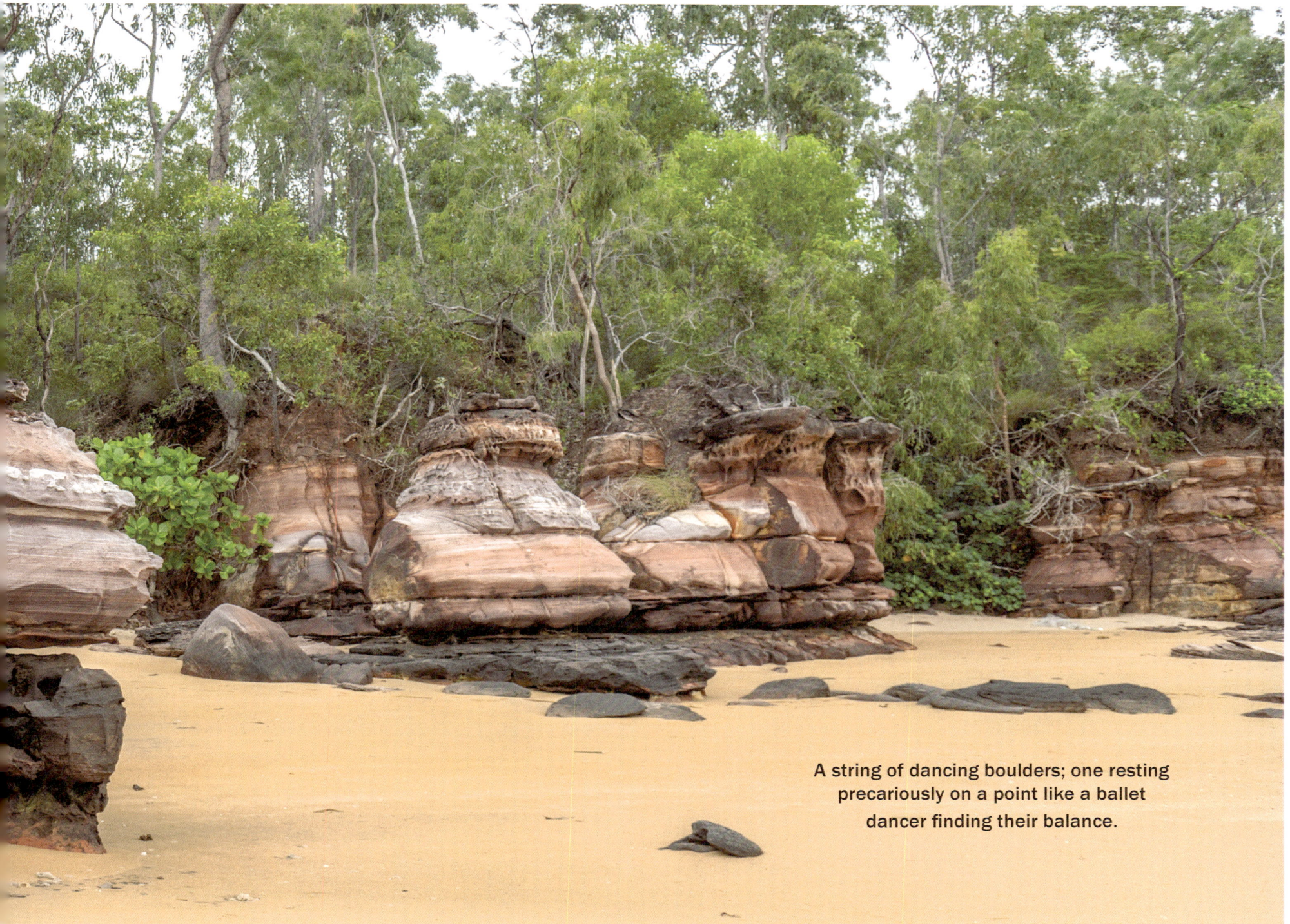

A string of dancing boulders; one resting precariously on a point like a ballet dancer finding their balance.

The footprints lead the eye to the cloud formation;
the greyness overtakes the scene, as the sun fades.

The large rock formation above the water line
takes on the form of a resting camel.

The visible intelligence of this
dingo as he pauses and stares,
his ears cocked, listening
intently to his surroundings.

As quietly as he appeared, the dingo slips away.

Step-by-step, manoeuvering through the rock formations, the subtle rise in the landscape is unnoticable as the rocks meet the clouds on the horizon. Revealing a portal that has opened, exposing a canvas of rich blue sky.

A tree branch resting on a rock contrasts sharply
with its surroundings, points the way back to the dwellings.

David Martinelli - Photographer/Author.

David resides in Toowoomba, (Queensland, Australia) with his wife Cathy of thirty two years. They have four adult children.

He is a photographer with a storytelling approach. A career spanning over forty years. His photography journey commenced in the mid 1980s. He has worked mainly in the editorial, wedding and portraiture fields.

The last fourteen years he worked as a photographer in higher educaiton, while still undertaking freelance work as a photojournalist.

This venture into landscape photography has been a recent endeavour.

This latest book joins a list of publications that have stemmed from personal projects.

This book is a result of an unforeseen opportunity. The images from this unique landscape, deserve to be shared for all to see.

www.ingramcontent.com/pod-product-compliance
Lightning Source LLC
Chambersburg PA
CBRC090735150426
42811CB00067B/1919

9 780994 312549